AF431800

Keto Air Fryer Cookbook

Easy and Delicious Low-Carb Recipes to Lose Weight and Heal Your Body

Melanie Bennet

Table of Contents

Introduction

If you plan to follow the keto diet, learning to prepare healthy ketogenic recipes is an important step toward achieving your goals. While you can cook keto-friendly foods in many ways, one method that's growing in popularity is using an air fryer. People have touted the air fryer as a "miraculous kitchen appliance." An air fryer can whip up crispy and flavorful foods in minutes.

From appetizers, snacks, and main courses, to dessert, there are many options for you to cook ketogenic meals in an air fryer. The more you learn to cook with your air fryer, the easier it becomes. Delicious air-fried dishes will keep your eating plan interesting and motivating. Easy to use, convenient, and versatile, air fryers are perfect for anyone on keto.

CHAPTER ONE

An Overview of the Ketogenic Diet

The ketogenic diet is a high-fat, low-carb diet similar to other low-carb diets, such as the Atkins diet. This diet focuses on significantly reducing the body's carbohydrate intake and substituting it with fat. As a result, the body enters a metabolic state known as ketosis. During this stage, the body becomes highly efficient at burning fat to make energy and converts the fat in the liver into ketones. In this phase, you won't experience the blood sugar spikes that cause that sluggish feeling a couple of hours after eating a high-carb meal. It is also in this stage that weight loss happens more quickly.

The daily nutritional intake on a ketogenic diet is:

65–75% of calories from Fat

25–30% from Protein

5–10% from Carbohydrates

Why Follow a Ketogenic Diet?

The biggest reason people follow a Ketogenic Diet is to lose weight and keep the weight off. If you've struggled with yo-yo dieting, as many people have, restricting carbs is a great way to end a vicious cycle. Since foods rich in fat tend to be satiating, their consumption in high amounts has the effect of reducing one's appetite. Studies show that people on low-carb diets tend to lose weight faster than those on low-fat diets. Weight loss comes with a long list of residual health benefits. You'll be at less risk for diabetes, high blood pressure, strokes, and heart attacks.

Most people who switch to a Ketogenic Diet report how their energy levels remain stable throughout the day. And the reason is simple—fat is a readily available energy source, which means the body can go for hours without food and not experience fluctuations in energy levels.

In addition to weight loss and a healthier lifestyle, this eating plan is also used to treat illnesses and chronic conditions. It has been effective for people battling epilepsy and children who have suffered from prolonged and dangerous seizures. It also helps achieve stable blood glucose levels, primarily due to the lack of carbohydrates and sugar in this diet.

The potential risks in a Ketogenic Diet are similar to those in any high-fat, low-carb diet. You're increasing the amount of fat you're eating, so if you're not significantly reducing your carbohydrate intake, you could negatively impact your body. If you have any pre-existing health conditions, talk to your doctor first before starting the Ketogenic Diet.

What to Eat on a Ketogenic Diet?

If you're considering trying a low carbohydrate diet, you may envision yourself eating large amounts of meat. But there are many other foods to choose from. In fact, making sure you eat plenty of vegetables is very important to your overall health and weight loss goals.

Meats: You can choose any kind of meat, including poultry, pork, beef, goat, lamb, and mutton. You can even eat the skin on the chicken!

Seafood and fish: You can eat any kind, but stick to the fattier kinds, such as mackerel, salmon, herring, and sardines.

Full-fat dairy products: Milk, yogurt, butter, cheeses, and sour cream.

Eggs

Nuts and seeds

Non-starchy vegetables: Cauliflower, asparagus, broccoli, zucchini, cabbage, tomatoes, squash, eggplants, leafy greens, Brussel sprouts, mushrooms, and onions

Fruits: Avocados are an absolute must. Berries can also be enjoyed often. Watch out for other fruits as they are higher in carbs.

Oils: Olive oil, flaxseed oil, avocado oil, coconut oil, and macadamia oil.

What to Avoid on a Ketogenic Diet?

Sugar: This is a keto dieter's worst enemy. You'll find sugar in most juices, soft drinks, cookies, cakes, and cereals.

Grains and products made from grains: Flour, pasta, baked goods, chips, wheat, and rice.

Starchy vegetables: Beans, potatoes, peas, lentils, parsnips, and corn.

Diet soda and fruit juices

Trans fats

CHAPTER TWO

Introduction to the Air Fryer

The key to following the ketogenic diet is to make things more interesting—and the best way to do this is by cooking your food in various ways. An air fryer will make it easier for you to stick with keto and enjoy keto-friendly meals.

The air fryer uses Rapid Air technology to cook foods. Foods are placed in the fryer's basket, and hot air is circulated rapidly around the ingredients. The air helps heat the food from all sides at once, which is precisely what happens when you deep fry foods using oil. The air fryer won't leave your kitchen with a greasy smell. This technology also ensures an optimal temperature is maintained within the fryer to avoid burning your food. The air fryer will make your food crispy on the outside and tender and tasty on the inside!

Benefits of Air Fryers

Air Fryer Saves You Time

Probably the most convenient thing about using an air fryer, this appliance is super time efficient. If you are a busy person (and who isn't nowadays?) and hate coming home just to spend your evening whisking in front of the stove, you will greatly appreciate having this appliance in your kitchen. But that's not all. Besides the fact that the air fryer can prepare delicious meals in a matter of minutes, what's even more impressive is how quickly it is to start cooking. Instead of waiting for a large amount of oil to heat up in the deep fryer, the air fryer can reach a temperature higher than 300 degrees F in an instant.

Air Fryer is an All-in-One Appliance

In addition to fried foods, you can grill, roast, and bake in an air fryer. You can prepare anything from Kentucky fried drumsticks to muffins, roasted veggies, and cakes. There is no need for other pans and pots because, with your air fryer, you will have everything you need to cook restaurant-grade meals.

Air Fryer is Easy to Clean
With an air fryer, there is no need for degreasing and scrubbing the sticky pots and pans after frying with oil. All parts are easily removable and can be washed in the dishwasher, which is convenient. Not to mention, switching to air frying means no more splatters all over your stove. I don't know about you, but I find that a huge plus.

Tips for Air Frying

Want to become a pro at air frying? Make sure to take advantage of the tips below to set your dinner table with meals that are fried to perfection.

Use a Cooking Spray
Although the air fryer manual says you don't need to add oil, you may still need oil to cook some foods, such as French fries. Otherwise, your food may stick to the fryer's surface. You can spray your air fryer with cooking oil or coat the food slightly with oil.

Do not Overcrowd the Air Fryer
It may be tempting to cook more food at once and have plenty of leftovers. However, remember that jam-packing your air fryer will lead to undercooked food, as the air doesn't have enough room to circulate.

Shake and Mix
When you cook using oil, the oil helps to mix your food properly, which cooks every little piece in the skillet or pan on all sides. This

does not happen in an air fryer since the air is not strong enough to separate the ingredients. To avoid undercooked food, you must open the machine at least once to shake the ingredients in the cooking basket. Most people remove the basket halfway through the cooking to shake the ingredients. For example, if you set a timer for 20 minutes, you would need to pause the fryer after 10 minutes and mix the ingredients before you restart the fryer again.

Check Your Food

Another great thing about the air fryer is that you can open the lid and check your food without disrupting the cooking process. Just like you open your oven to see whether your food is cooked to perfection, you can do the same with the air fryer.

Make an Aluminum Sling

One thing I find challenging about this appliance is getting the cooked food out of it. To make your cooking process a lot easier, make an aluminum sling and put it underneath the baking pan. I suggest a sling that is 24 inches long and 2 inches wide. Now, when cooking is done, you can easily lift your pan with the help of this sling.

Add Some Water

Sometimes, especially when cooking super fatty ingredients (think bacon), the grease inside the Air Fryer can start smoking. This is normal and nothing to worry about; however, if you want to avoid this, I suggest adding just a bit of water underneath the basket.

Start with Room Temperature

When you cook using fresh ingredients, do not start cooking them immediately after taking them out of the fridge. Let the ingredients warm to room temperature before placing them in the fryer. This will reduce the cooking time and will also give you crispier results.

Do More with It

Although this appliance is called an air "fryer," it does much more than just frying food. You can make anything from noodles to a pizza in an air fryer. An air fryer has more in common with a fan-forced oven than a deep fryer. You can roast, bake, and grill in an air fryer. In other words, experiment!

Take Good Care of Your Air Fryer

To take good care of your air fryer, you don't have to clean it constantly, but like every other electronic appliance, it does need a certain level of care. If you use your air fryer regularly, you will need to clean it every five to ten days to prevent unwanted smells. Use a dishwasher to clean the removable parts of the fryer or soak them in soapy water before washing them gently with a sponge.

CHAPTER THREE

Breakfast Recipes

Breakfast is the most important meal of the day. Here are some simple and tasty keto recipes for you to try.

Mini Breakfast Egg Cups

Yield: 8 mini egg cups

Ingredients:

- 2 tablespoons milk or heavy whipping cream
- ¼ cup of green peppers (chopped)
- ¼ cup of mozzarella cheese (shredded)
- ¼ cup of onions (chopped)
- ¼ cup of red peppers (chopped)
- ¼ cup of spinach (fresh, chopped)
- ½ cup of cheddar cheese (shredded)
- 3 slices of bacon (cooked, crumbled)
- 6 large eggs
- Salt and pepper to taste

Directions:

1. In a bowl, add the eggs, milk, pepper, and salt, then whisk well to combine.

2. Add half of the green peppers, mozzarella cheese, onions, red peppers, spinach, cheddar cheese, and crumbled bacon, and continue whisking to combine.

3. In a separate bowl, combine the rest of the ingredients and mix well.

4. Preheat your air fryer at 320°F for about 3 minutes.

5. Place a silicone muffin mold in your air fryer. Doing this before pouring in the egg mixture is easier than trying to place a filled muffin mold into the air fryer without spilling anything.

6. Spray the molds with cooking spray, then pour the egg mixture into each mold.

7. Sprinkle the combined ingredients over each of the egg cups.

8. Close your air fryer and cook the mini egg cups for 12 to 15 minutes. You may check the doneness after 12 minutes by inserting a toothpick into one of the egg cups. If it comes out clean, it means the eggs have been cooked.

9. Take the egg cups out of your air fryer and allow them to cool slightly before removing them from the molds. Serve immediately.

Baked Avocado Egg

Yield: 2 servings

Ingredients:

- 1 tablespoon parsley (fresh, chopped)
- 1 large avocado
- 2 small eggs
- Salt and pepper to taste
- ¼ cup of cheddar cheese (shredded, optional)

Directions:

1. Preheat your air fryer at 400°F for about 3 minutes.
2. Cut the avocado in half and take the pit out.
3. Place the avocados face-up on a plate.
4. Crack the eggs into each of the avocado slices. Do this carefully to ensure that the yolks remain intact. Sprinkle with pepper and salt to taste, and top each avocado egg with cheddar cheese if desired.
5. Place the avocado eggs in your air fryer and cook for about 12 to 15 minutes. After 12 minutes, check the doneness of the egg. You may continue cooking if you want the eggs to be well-done.
6. Once cooked, take the avocado eggs out of the air fryer, top with fresh parsley, and serve immediately.

Breakfast Roll-Ups

Yield: 2 breakfast roll-ups

Ingredients:

- 2 tablespoons butter
- ⅓ cup of salsa (mild or hot)
- ½ cup of green bell peppers (chopped)
- ½ cup of onions (chopped)
- ⅔ cup of cheddar cheese (shredded)
- 4 large eggs
- 6 slices of bacon (sugar-free)
- Salt and pepper to taste

Directions:

1. In a skillet, melt the butter over medium heat.

2. Add the green bell peppers and onions and cook to soften, about 3 minutes.

3. In a bowl, whisk the eggs with a dash of pepper and salt to taste.

4. Add the eggs to the skillet, then mix together to scramble.

5. While the eggs are still a bit undercooked, take the skillet off the heat. They should be cooked enough to hold their form but not too cooked as they will continue cooking when placed in the air fryer.

6. On a plate, lay 3 slices of bacon next to each other.

7. Transfer half of the egg mixture onto one side of the bacon slices. Top with half of the cheddar cheese.

8. Gently roll the bacon slices around the eggs and cheese, then use a toothpick to secure the breakfast roll-up.

9. Repeat the same steps using the rest of the bacon, egg mixture, and cheese.

10. Preheat your air fryer at 350°F for about 3 minutes.

11. Place the breakfast roll-ups in your air fryer's basket and cook for about 15 minutes.

12.	Halfway through the cooking time, flip the breakfast roll-ups over to cook evenly.

13.	Once cooked, transfer the breakfast roll-ups to plates and serve immediately with a side of salsa.

Quick Breakfast Frittata

Yield: 10 servings

Ingredients:

- 4 cherry tomatoes (halved)
- 1 cup sausage (crumbled)
- 4 large eggs
- 1 tablespoon olive oil
- 4 tablespoons fresh parsley (chopped)
- ½ cup parmesan cheese (grated)
- Salt and pepper to taste

Directions:

1. Preheat the air fryer to 390°F.

2. Insert a small pan and put the cherry tomatoes and crumbled sausage in the pan.

3. Cook for 6–7 minutes.

4. In a bowl, whisk together the eggs, parsley, cheese, salt, and pepper.

5. Pour the egg mixture over the tomatoes and sausage.

6. Bake in the air fryer for 5–6 more minutes.

Crispy Bacon

Yield: 12 slices

Ingredients:

- 12 slices of bacon (thick-cut, sugar-free)

Directions:

1. Set your air fryer's temperature to 400°F and preheat for about 3 minutes.

2. Place the slices of bacon in your air fryer's basket. If needed, cook the bacon slices in batches.

3. Cook the slices of bacon for about 10 minutes. If you're using thinner slices, you may have a shorter cooking time.

4. Halfway through the cooking time, turn the bacon slices or give the basket a shake to rearrange them.

5. After 10 minutes, check the crispness of your bacon. If you want it to be extra crispy, continue cooking for 1 or 2 minutes more.

6. If cooking more than one batch, remove the grease from the lower basket before moving on to the next batch.

7. Enjoy your bacon while hot and pair it with scrambled eggs for the perfect breakfast treat.

Cheese Omelet

Yield: 1 serving
Ingredients:

- 2 large eggs
- 1 onion (diced)
- ⅛ teaspoon hot sauce
- ¼ cup cheddar cheese (grated)
- Salt and pepper to taste

Directions:

1. Preheat the air fryer to 360°F.

2. In a bowl, whisk the eggs until fluffy, and stir in the hot sauce, salt, and pepper.

3. Place a small pan inside the air fryer and spray with a non-stick cooking spray.

4. Put the onions in the pan and cook for 10 minutes.

5. Pour the whisked eggs over the onions and top with the cheddar cheese.

6. Cook the omelet for another 5 minutes.

Soufflé

Yield: 2 servings

Ingredients:

- 2 eggs
- 2 tablespoons cream
- 1 tablespoon red pepper flakes
- 1 tablespoon fresh parsley (chopped)

Directions:

1. Preheat the air fryer to 400°F.

2. In a bowl, combine eggs with cream, red pepper flakes, and parsley. Pour into two soufflé cups and set in the air fryer.

3. Cook for 5 minutes if you want soft eggs and 8 minutes if you prefer hard eggs.

CHAPTER FOUR

Snacks and Appetizers

Even following a restrictive diet like keto, you can enjoy snacks and appetizers—as long as they are low-carb, high-fat, and have moderate amounts of protein. The great thing about making your snacks and appetizers in an air fryer is that you can have them ready in no time.

Mozzarella Sticks

Yield: 2 servings

Ingredients:

- ½ teaspoon salt
- 2½ teaspoons of Italian seasoning blend
- 1 tablespoon parsley (fresh, chopped)
- 2 tablespoons Parmesan cheese (grated)
- ½ cup of almond flour
- 1 large egg
- 3 mozzarella cheese sticks (cut lengthwise)
- cooking spray

Directions:

1. After slicing the cheese, place it in the freezer to harden overnight.

2. Preheat your air fryer at 370°F for about 3 minutes.

3. In a bowl, crack the egg and beat it well.

4. In a second bowl, combine the almond flour, Italian seasoning blend, salt, and Parmesan cheese, then mix until well incorporated.

5. Take the mozzarella cheese sticks out of the freezer and dip them in the beaten egg, one at a time.

6. Dredge each of the mozzarella cheese sticks in the flour mixture, making sure you have coated them evenly.

7. Place them on a plate or wire rack after coating and grease lightly with cooking spray.

8. Place the mozzarella sticks in your air fryer's basket and cook for about 5 minutes.

9. Halfway through the cooking time, shake the basket or flip the mozzarella cheese sticks individually.

10.   Once cooked, transfer the mozzarella cheese sticks to a plate, sprinkle with parsley, and serve while hot.

Zucchini Fries

Yield: 4 servings

Ingredients:

- 1 teaspoon Italian seasoning blend
- ½ cup of almond flour
- ½ cup of Parmesan cheese (grated)
- 1 large egg (beaten)
- 2 medium-sized zucchinis
- Salt and pepper to taste
- Cooking spray
- ½ teaspoon garlic powder (optional)

Directions:

1. Cut the zucchinis in half, then slice them further to make fries. Ideally, they will be 3 to 4 inches long and ½-inch thick.

2. In a bowl, crack the egg and beat well.

3. In a second bowl, combine the almond flour, Italian seasoning, Parmesan cheese, and a dash of salt and pepper, then mix well to combine. Add garlic powder, too, if desired.

4. Dip the zucchini fries in the egg, one at a time.

5. Dredge the zucchini fries in the flour mixture, making sure you have coated them evenly.

6. Place the zucchini fries on a plate or wire rack after coating and grease lightly with cooking spray.

7. Preheat your air fryer at 400°F for about 3 minutes.

8. Place the zucchini fries in your air fryer's basket in a single layer. Cook in batches if needed.

9. Cook the zucchini fries for about 10 minutes until crispy.

10. Halfway through the cooking time, shake the basket or flip the zucchini fries individually.

11. Once cooked, transfer the zucchini fries to a plate and serve while hot.

Easy Buffalo Ranch Chicken Wings

Yield: 4 servings

Ingredients:

- 1 pound chicken wings, drums, and flats
- 1 tablespoon Frank's RedHot (cayenne pepper sauce)
- ¼ cup ranch dressing

Directions:

1. Preheat your air fryer to 390°F.
2. Put the wings in the fryer basket and cook for 15 minutes.
3. Give it a shake at the halfway mark.
4. Pour into a bowl and cover with wing sauce and ranch.

Sausage-Stuffed Mushrooms

Yield: 8 servings

Ingredients:

- 1 cup of cream cheese (softened)
- 1 cup of mushroom stems (chopped)
- mushroom caps
- 1 cup of spinach (chopped)
- 1 lb pork sausage (hot or mild, sliced)
- Cooking spray

Directions:

1. In a skillet, brown the sausage slices over medium heat. Once browned, drain the oil and transfer the pork sausage to a bowl.

2. Add the cream cheese to the bowl over the hot sausage slices.

3. In the same skillet, sauté the mushroom stems until softened.

4. Add the spinach and continue sautéing for 2 more minutes.

5. Take the skillet off the heat and add the spinach-mushroom mixture to the bowl with the sausage slices and cream cheese.

6. Mix until all of the ingredients are well incorporated.

7. Spoon the mixture into the mushroom caps, place them on a rack, and grease lightly with cooking spray.

8. Preheat your air fryer at 390°F for about 3 minutes.

9. Place the stuffed mushroom caps in your air fryer's basket in a single layer. If needed, cook in batches.

10. Cook the stuffed mushroom caps for 8 minutes.

11. Halfway through, check for doneness. You may continue cooking for a couple more minutes until golden brown and bubbly.

12. Once cooked, transfer the stuffed mushroom caps to a plate and serve immediately.

Chicken Nuggets

Yield: 6 servings

Ingredients:

- ½ teaspoon garlic powder
- ½ teaspoon salt
- 1 teaspoon onion flakes
- 4 tablespoons of olive or coconut oil
- ½ cup of almond flour
- 2 lbs chicken breast (chopped into nuggets)
- 1 egg (whisked)

Directions:

1. Mix the egg and oil in a bowl, and then use a fork to mix well.

2. In a second bowl, combine the almond flour, garlic powder, salt, and onion flakes, then mix well.

3. Dip each of the chicken nuggets into the egg mixture.

4. Dredge each of the chicken nuggets in the flour mixture, making sure they are evenly coated.

5. Place the nuggets on a plate or wire rack after coating and grease lightly with cooking spray.

6. Preheat your air fryer at 360°F for about 3 minutes.

7. Place the chicken nuggets in your air fryer's basket in a single layer. Cook in batches if needed.

8. Cook the zucchini fries for about 10 to 15 minutes until crispy.

9. Halfway through the cooking time, shake the basket or flip the chicken nuggets individually.

10. Once cooked, transfer the chicken nuggets to a plate and serve while hot.

Cajun Shrimp

Yield: 2 servings

Ingredients:

- 16 large shrimps (peeled and deveined)
- 1 tablespoon celery salt
- ¼ teaspoon cayenne pepper
- ¼ teaspoon paprika
- Dash of dry mustard
- Dash of cinnamon
- Salt and pepper to taste
- 1 tablespoon olive oil

Directions:

1. Preheat the air fryer to 380°F.
2. In a bowl, mix all of the spices and the oil.
3. Coat the shrimp thoroughly with the spice mix.
4. Cook the shrimp for 5 minutes.
5. Serve hot.

Cheesy Jalapeño Poppers

Yield: 3 servings

Ingredients:
- ½ teaspoon garlic powder
- ⅓ cup of cheddar cheese (shredded)
- ½ cup of cream cheese
- 6 jalapeño peppers
- 12 slices of bacon (uncured, thin-cut)
- Cooking spray
- Ranch dressing (optional, for dipping)

Directions:

1. Cut each jalapeño pepper in half, then scoop out the ribs and seeds. Wash your hands thoroughly after this step.

2. In a bowl, combine the garlic powder, cheddar cheese, and cream cheese, then mix until well incorporated.

3. Scoop the filling into the jalapeño pepper halves.

4. Wrap each of the stuffed jalapeño pepper halves with a slice of bacon. Start wrapping from the bottom, then tuck the ends in when you're done. Doing this prevents the bacon from shrinking and keeps the filling from oozing out.

5. Preheat your air fryer at 350°F for about 3 minutes.

6. Spray the stuffed jalapeño pepper halves with cooking spray and place them in your air fryer's basket. Cook in batches if needed.

7. Cook the stuffed jalapeño pepper halves for about 15 minutes. Halfway through the cooking time, flip the stuffed jalapeño pepper halves over.

8. After 15 minutes, increase the temperature to 400°F, then continue cooking until the bacon becomes crispy, about 3 to 4 more minutes.

9. Once cooked, transfer the stuffed jalapeño pepper halves to a plate and serve with ranch dressing if desired.

CHAPTER FIVE

Poultry

Poultry can be prepared in so many ways—and when you have an air fryer, cooking poultry becomes even more enjoyable. Here are a few keto-friendly poultry recipes to practice with your air fryer.

Fried Chicken

Yield: 6 servings
Ingredients:
- ¼ teaspoon black pepper
- ¼ teaspoon thyme (dried)
- ½ teaspoon garlic powder
- ½ teaspoon sea salt
- 1 teaspoon smoked paprika
- ¼ cup of coconut flour
- 1 cup of pork rinds (crushed)
- 2½ lbs chicken (drumsticks)
- 2 large eggs
- Cooking spray

Directions:
1. In a bowl, combine the coconut flour, pepper, and salt, then mix well.

2. In a second bowl, crack the eggs and whisk them together.

3. In a third bowl, combine the garlic powder, thyme, pork rinds, and smoked paprika, then mix well.

4. Start coating the chicken drumsticks by dredging them in the flour mixture first.

5. Then dip each of the chicken drumsticks into the egg mixture. Shake off any excess.

6. Finally, dredge the drumsticks in the pork rind mixture, then place them on a plate or wire rack. To avoid clumping, you can use the pork rind mixture little by little. Divide the mixture between two bowls: one for dredging and one for refilling.

7. Preheat your air fryer at 400°F for about 5 minutes.

8. Lightly grease the coated chicken drumsticks with cooking spray.

9. Place the chicken drumsticks in your air fryer's basket in a single layer. Make sure there are spaces between each of the drumsticks. If needed, cook in batches.

10. Cook the chicken for about 20 minutes, until its internal temperature reaches 165°F. Halfway through the cooking time, turn the drumsticks over to ensure they cook evenly.

11. Once cooked, transfer the fried chicken drumsticks to a plate and serve while hot and crispy.

Savory Tandoori Chicken

Yield: 4 servings

Ingredients for the chicken:

- ½ teaspoon cayenne pepper
- 1 teaspoon garam masala
- 1 teaspoon salt
- 1 teaspoon smoked paprika
- 1 teaspoon turmeric
- 1 tablespoon garlic (minced)
- 1 tablespoon ginger (minced)
- ¼ cup of cilantro
- ¼ cup of Greek yogurt
- 1 lb chicken tenders (cut in half)

Ingredients for finishing:

- 2 teaspoons lemon juice (freshly squeezed, for finishing)
- 1 tablespoon olive oil (for basting)
- 2 tablespoons cilantro (fresh, chopped, for garnishing)

Directions:

1. In a bowl, combine all the chicken ingredients and toss until well combined.

2. Allow marinating for at least 30 minutes. The longer you leave it, the more flavorful your chicken will be.

3. Preheat your air fryer at 350°F for about 5 minutes.

4. Place the marinated chicken tenders in your air fryer's basket in a single layer. If needed, cook the chicken tenders in batches.

5. Use a silicone brush to baste the chicken tenders with olive oil.

6. Cook the chicken tenders for about 10 minutes.

7. Flip the chicken tenders over, baste the other side, then continue cooking for 5 more minutes.

8. Use a meat thermometer to check the internal temperature of the chicken tenders. You know that they are cooked through when the internal temperature reaches 165°F.

9. Once cooked, transfer the tandoori chicken tenders to a plate.

10.   Drizzle with lemon juice and toss lightly to coat.

11.   Garnish with fresh cilantro before serving.

Crusty Turkey Breast

Yield: 4 servings

Ingredients:

- 1 teaspoon sage (dried)
- 1 teaspoon thyme (dried)
- ½ tablespoon poultry seasoning (keto-friendly)
- 2 tablespoons olive oil
- 4 lbs turkey breast (bone-in)
- Salt and pepper to taste

Directions:

1. Grease the turkey breast by rubbing olive oil all over it.

2. Sprinkle the turkey breast with salt, pepper, and poultry seasoning, then rub the seasonings all over to make them stick.

3. Preheat your air fryer at 350°F for about 5 minutes.

4. Place the turkey breast in your air fryer's basket, skin-side down.

5. Cook the turkey breast for about 25 minutes.

6. Flip the turkey breast over, then cook for another 20 to 30 minutes.

7. Use a meat thermometer to test the internal temperature of the turkey breast. Place the thermometer in the thickest part of the meat to ensure the internal temperature reaches 160°F. This means it has already cooked all the way through.

8. Once cooked, transfer the turkey breast to a wire rack and allow to rest for 10 to 15 minutes before slicing and serving.

Crispy Chicken Wings

Yield: 6 servings

Ingredients:

- 3 pounds chicken wings
- 2 tablespoons olive oil
- 2 tablespoons dark soy sauce
- 6 garlic cloves (finely chopped)
- 4 jalapeno peppers (finely chopped)
- 1 tablespoon allspice powder
- 1 teaspoon cinnamon powder
- 1 teaspoon cayenne pepper powder
- 1 teaspoon white pepper powder
- 1 teaspoon salt
- 1 tablespoon fresh thyme (finely chopped)
- 1 tablespoon fresh ginger (grated)
- 4 scallions (finely chopped)
- 5 tablespoons lime juice
- ½ cup red wine vinegar

Directions:

1. In a large bowl, add chicken wings and all the other ingredients except for olive oil. Mix until well combined.

2. Marinate for 24 hours in the fridge.

3. Preheat the air fryer to 390°F.

4. Use a paper towel to pat chicken wings dry. Brush olive oil onto the wings.

5. Add wings to the basket and set the time to 15 minutes.

6. Shake the basket at the 7-and-a-half-minute mark to distribute the wings in the basket.

7. Check at the 15-minute mark if the wings are crispy enough. If not, fry for 4 more minutes.

8. Serve hot.

Jerk Chicken Drumsticks

Yield: 4 servings

Ingredients:

- 1 pound chicken drumsticks
- 2 tablespoons olive oil
- 2 tablespoons freshly squeezed lime juice
- 4 green onions (chopped)
- 2 habanero chiles (seeds and stems removed and minced)
- 3 garlic cloves (minced)
- 1 tablespoon dried thyme
- ½ tablespoon dried ginger

Directions:

1. Combine all the ingredients in a bowl and marinate the chicken drumsticks the night before you plan to cook this recipe.

2. When you're ready to cook, preheat your air fryer to 390°F.

3. Place the drumsticks in the fryer and cook for 10 minutes.

4. Lower the heat to 350°F and cook for another 10 minutes. You should have a crispy and caramelized exterior on your chicken.

5. Serve hot.

Chicken Tandoori

Yield: 4 servings

Ingredients:

- 4 chicken thighs
- Salt and pepper to taste
- ½ teaspoon chili paste
- ½ teaspoon garlic paste
- ¼ teaspoon garam masala powder
- ¼ teaspoon coriander
- ¼ teaspoon cumin
- 1 teaspoon lime juice
- 2 tablespoons plain Greek yogurt
- 1 teaspoon olive oil

Directions:

1. Use a sharp knife to score the chicken thighs in several places.

2. Combine all other ingredients except for the olive oil in a bowl.

3. Thoroughly coat the chicken with the spice mix and refrigerate for a few hours.

4. Preheat the air fryer to 380°F.

5. Add the chicken thighs and cook for 10 minutes.

6. Remove the chicken from the basket and brush with the olive oil.

7. Return chicken to the air fryer and cook for 5 more minutes.

8. Serve while hot.

CHAPTER SIX

Meats

The air fryer is a versatile kitchen appliance that can create various tasty and keto-friendly dishes. Following are some meat dishes to increase the intake of protein and healthy fats in your keto meal plan.

Garlic Butter Steak

Yield: 2 servings

Ingredients for the steaks:

- 2 ribeye steaks (about ¼ lb each)
- Salt and pepper to taste
- Olive oil

Ingredients for the garlic butter:

- ½ teaspoon salt
- 1 teaspoon Worcestershire sauce
- 2 teaspoons garlic (minced)
- 2 tablespoons parsley (fresh, chopped)
- 1 stick butter (unsalted, softened)

Directions:

1. In a bowl, combine the garlic butter ingredients and mix until well incorporated.

2. Transfer to a piece of parchment paper and carefully roll the sauce into a log.

3. Place the garlic butter log in the refrigerator until ready to serve.

4. Place the steaks on a plate and allow them to warm to room temperature.

5. Grease each of the steaks with olive oil on both sides. Season with salt and pepper all over, as well.

6. Preheat your air fryer at 400°F for about 5 minutes.

7. Place one steak in your air fryer and cook for about 12 minutes. Halfway through the cooking time, flip the steak over to cook evenly.

8. Once cooked, place the steak on a new plate and allow it to rest. Repeat the steps for the other steak.

9. Before serving, top each steak with chilled slices of garlic butter.

Asian Steak

Yield: 4 servings

Ingredients:

- 1 pound steak
- 1 cup cilantro leaves (finely chopped)
- ¼ cup mint leaves (finely chopped)
- 2 tablespoons oregano leaves (finely chopped)
- 3 garlic cloves (finely chopped)
- 1 teaspoon red pepper powder
- 1 tablespoon cumin powder
- 1 teaspoon cayenne pepper powder
- 2 teaspoons smoked paprika powder
- Salt to taste
- ¼ teaspoon black pepper
- 1 tablespoon olive oil
- 3 tablespoons red wine vinegar

Directions:

1. Add cilantro leaves, mint leaves, oregano leaves, cloves, pepper powder, cumin powder, cayenne pepper, paprika, salt, and pepper to a bowl along with oil and vinegar, and mix until well combined.

2. Cut steak into small pieces. Add steak to the herb mixture and marinate in the fridge for 2 to 24 hours.

3. Preheat the air fryer to 390°F.

4. Pat steak dry using tissues. Place in the basket and fry for 10 to 12 minutes or until desired doneness.

5. Serve with a sauce of your choice.

Spicy Lamb Steak

Yield: 4 servings

Ingredients:

- ½ teaspoon cardamom (ground)
- 1 teaspoon cayenne pepper
- 1 teaspoon cinnamon (ground)
- 1 teaspoon fennel (ground)
- 1 teaspoon garam masala
- 1 teaspoon salt
- 1 lb lamb sirloin steaks (boneless)
- ½ onion (sliced)
- 4 ginger slices
- 5 cloves of garlic

Directions:

1. In a blender, combine all of the ingredients except the lamb.

2. Blend until the onions have been finely minced and all ingredients are well incorporated. This may take about 3 to 4 minutes.

3. In a bowl, add the lamb steaks. With a knife, slice all over the meat and fat without cutting all the way through. This allows the meat to absorb the marinade more effectively.

4. Add the spice paste into the bowl and toss lightly until the steaks are evenly coated.

5. Place the bowl in the refrigerator and allow to rest for a minimum of 30 minutes. The longer, the better—you can even marinate the steaks for up to 24 hours.

6. When ready to cook, preheat your air fryer at 350°F for about 5 minutes.

7. Place the steaks on your air fryer in a single layer, with spaces in between. If needed, cook in batches.

8. Cook the steaks for about 15 minutes. Halfway through the cooking time, flip the steaks to cook them evenly.

9. Use a meat thermometer to check the internal temperature of the steaks. You know they are done if the internal temperature reaches 150°F.

10.   Once cooked, transfer the steaks to a plate and serve immediately.

Crispy Pork Belly

Yield: 4 servings

Ingredients:

- 1 teaspoon black pepper
- 1 teaspoon salt
- 2 tablespoons soy sauce
- 3 cups of water
- 1 lb pork belly
- 2 bay leaves
- 6 cloves of garlic
- Cooking spray

Directions:

1. Slice the pork belly into 3 thick pieces to allow for even cooking.

2. If you have a pressure cooker, place the pork belly slices into it, along with all of the other ingredients.

3. Cook the pork belly slices on high for about 15 minutes.

4. After cooking, leave the pot for about 10 minutes before releasing the remaining pressure.

5. Use a pair of tongs to transfer the pork belly slices to a wire rack. Allow resting for about 10 minutes.

6. If you don't have a pressure cooker, you can place everything in a saucepan. Cover with a lid and cook over medium heat for 60 minutes. You'll know the pork belly is cooked when you can easily slide a knife into the skin side.

7. Use a pair of tongs to transfer the pork belly slices to a wire rack. Allow resting for about 10 minutes.

8. Once cool, cut the pork belly slices in half and grease them lightly with cooking spray.

9. Preheat your air fryer at 400°F for about 5 minutes.

10. Place the pork belly slices in your air fryer's basket.

11.   Cook the pork belly slices for about 15 minutes. Halfway through the cooking time, flip the pork belly slices to cook them evenly.

12.   Once cooked and crispy, transfer the pork belly slices to a plate and serve while hot.

Barbeque Pork

Yield: 4 servings

Ingredients:

- 4 pieces of pork loin (6-8 ounces each)
- 2 tablespoons balsamic vinegar
- 1 tablespoon soy sauce
- 1 tablespoon tomato paste
- 1 clove garlic (minced)
- 1 teaspoon fresh ginger (grated)
- Salt and pepper to taste

Directions:

1. Season the pork with salt and pepper.
2. Put the vinegar, soy sauce, tomato paste, and garlic in a bowl and whisk. Add the ginger and marinate the pork for 30 minutes.
3. Preheat your air fryer to 350°F.
4. Cook the pork on the baking tray of your fryer for 8 minutes, then flip them to cook on the other side for another 8 minutes.

Steak Kebabs

Yield: 4 servings

Ingredients:

- ¼ teaspoon black pepper
- ½ teaspoon cumin (ground)
- 1 tablespoon garlic (minced)
- ¼ cup of olive oil
- ¼ cup of soy sauce
- 1 cup baby bella mushrooms (stems removed)
- 1 lb sirloin steak (cut into chunks about 1-inch thick)
- 1 green bell pepper (sliced for skewering)
- 1 red onion (sliced for skewering)
- Salt to taste

Directions:

1. In a bowl, combine the chunks of steak, black pepper, cumin, garlic, olive oil, soy sauce, and salt, then toss well to coat evenly.

2. Allow the chunks of steak to marinate for a minimum of 30 minutes.

3. After marinating, place the green pepper, red onion, mushrooms, and meat chunks on skewers.

4. Preheat your air fryer at 400°F for about 5 minutes.

5. Place the skewers in your air fryer and cook them for about 10 to 12 minutes. Halfway through the cooking time, flip the skewers to cook evenly.

6. Once cooked, transfer the steak kebabs to a plate and serve immediately.

Meatloaf Sliders

Yield: 8 servings
Ingredients:
- ½ teaspoon black pepper
- ½ teaspoon sea salt
- ½ teaspoon tarragon (dried)
- 1 teaspoon Italian seasoning
- 1 tablespoon Worcestershire sauce
- ¼ cup of coconut flour
- ¼ cup of keto ketchup
- ¼ cup of onions (finely chopped)
- ½ cup of almond flour (blanched, extra fine)
- 1 lb ground beef
- 1 clove of garlic (minced)
- 2 eggs (beaten)

Directions:
1. In a bowl, combine the ingredients and use your hands to mix everything together.

2. Still using your hands, shape the mixture into patties that have a thickness of 1 inch and are 2 inches in diameter. You can make bigger or smaller patties as long as you make them roughly the same size, so they cook evenly.

3. Transfer the patties to a plate and place them in the refrigerator to firm up for a minimum of 10 minutes.

4. Preheat your air fryer at 360°F for about 5 minutes.

5. Place the patties in your air fryer's basket in a single layer. If needed, cook in batches.

6. Cook the patties for about 10 minutes. Halfway through the cooking time, flip the patties to cook evenly.

Middle Eastern Meatballs

Yield: 6 servings

Ingredients:

- 1 pound ground lamb
- 4 ounces ground chicken
- 1½ tablespoons cilantro (finely chopped)
- 1 tablespoon mint (finely chopped)
- 1 teaspoon cumin powder
- 1 teaspoon coriander powder
- 1 teaspoon cayenne pepper powder
- 1 teaspoon red chili paste
- 2 garlic cloves (finely chopped)
- ¼ cup olive oil
- 1 teaspoon salt
- 1 egg white

Directions:

1. Preheat the air fryer to 390°F.

2. Add lamb, chicken, cilantro, mint, cumin, coriander, cayenne, red chili, and garlic to a bowl and mix until well combined.

3. Add egg whites to a bowl along with salt and mix well. Pour this into the meat mixture and combine into a dough.

4. Roll out small balls from the mixture.

5. Apply some oil to the surface of the meatballs and place them in the basket.

6. Lower heat to 360°F and cook meatballs for 6 to 8 minutes or until golden on all sides.

7. Serve with mint chutney.

Sausage and Peppers

Yield: 3 servings

Ingredients:

- 6 Italian sausages (hot or sweet)
- 1 red bell pepper (sliced into strips)
- 1 green bell pepper (sliced into strips)
- 1 small red onion (cut into chunks)
- 1 package sauerkraut (16 ounces)
- ¼ cup mustard

Directions:

1. Preheat your air fryer to 350°F.
2. Cut up the pepper and onion strips and set them aside.
3. Arrange the sausages in the air fryer basket and cook for 5 minutes. Give them a toss to ensure browning on all sides and prevent sticking, and cover with the peppers and onions. Cook for another 5 minutes.
4. Serve with the sauerkraut and mustard.

CHAPTER SEVEN

Fish and Seafood

Fish and seafood can be pretty challenging to cook if you're not used to handling them. Cooking fish and seafood is much easier when you use an air fryer.

Fish Sticks

Yield: 4 servings

Ingredients:
- 2 tablespoons Dijon mustard
- 2 tablespoons water
- ¼ cup of mayonnaise
- ¾ cup of Cajun seasoning
- 1½ cups pork rind (crushed)
- 1 lb white fish fillets (like cod, tilapia, catfish, and others)
- Salt and pepper to taste
- Cooking spray

Directions:
1. Pat the fish fillets dry, cut them into sticks, and set aside.
2. In a bowl, combine the mustard, mayonnaise, and water, then whisk well.
3. In a second bowl, combine the crushed pork rinds with the Cajun seasoning. Season with salt and pepper as needed. You may have to taste the mixture to determine how much salt and pepper to add.
4. Dip the fish sticks into the mustard mixture one at a time.
5. Then, dredge the fish sticks one by one into the pork rind mixture, making sure you have coated each fish stick evenly.

6. Place the coated fish sticks on a plate and grease lightly with cooking spray.

7. Preheat your air fryer at 400°F for about 3 minutes.

8. Place the coated fish sticks in your air fryer's basket in a single layer. If needed, cook in batches.

9. Cook the fish sticks for about 10 minutes. Halfway through the cooking time, flip the fish sticks to cook evenly.

10.	Once cooked, transfer the fish sticks to a plate and serve hot with a keto-friendly dipping sauce of your choice.

Spiced Salmon

Yield: 2 servings

Ingredients:

- 2 teaspoons avocado oil
- 2 teaspoons paprika
- 2 salmon fillets (wild-caught)
- Salt and pepper to taste
- 4 lemon wedges (for garnishing)

Directions:

1. Place the salmon fillets on a plate and allow them to warm to room temperature.

2. Cover the fillets with olive oil, paprika, salt, and pepper, then rub gently to coat evenly.

3. Preheat your air fryer at 390°F for about 3 minutes.

4. Place the salmon fillets in your air fryer's basket and cook them for 7 to 8 minutes. Halfway through the cooking time, flip the salmon fillets to cook evenly.

5. Once cooked, transfer the salmon to serving plates, garnish with lemon wedges, and serve.

Scallops with Tomato-Basil Sauce

Yield: 2 servings

Ingredients:

- ½ teaspoon black pepper
- ½ teaspoon salt
- 1 teaspoon garlic (minced)
- 1 tablespoon basil (fresh, chopped)
- 1 tablespoon tomato paste
- ¾ cup of heavy whipping cream
- 1½ cups of spinach (rinsed, drained)
- 8 large sea scallops
- Cooking spray

Directions:

1. In a heatproof pan that fits inside your air fryer, spread out the spinach to create an even layer at the bottom.

2. Lightly coat the scallops with cooking spray and season with salt and pepper.

3. Place the seasoned scallops on top of the layer of spinach.

4. In a bowl, combine the whipping cream, garlic, basil, tomato paste, salt, and pepper, then mix well.

5. Pour the sauce over the scallops and spinach.

6. Preheat your air fryer at 350°F for about 3 minutes.

7. Place the pan in your air fryer and cook the scallops for about 10 minutes. Use a cooking thermometer to check their internal temperature. You'll know the scallops are cooked when the internal temperature reaches 135°F, and the sauce starts bubbling.

8. Take the pan out of your air fryer and serve immediately.

Garlic Parmesan Shrimp

Yield: 2 servings

Ingredients:

- ½ teaspoon oregano (dried)
- 1 teaspoon basil (dried)
- 1 teaspoon black pepper
- 1 teaspoon onion powder
- 2 tablespoons olive oil
- ⅔ cup of Parmesan cheese (grated)
- 2 lbs jumbo shrimps (cooked, peeled, deveined)
- 1 lemon (quartered)
- 4 cloves of garlic (minced)

Directions:

1. In a bowl, combine the oregano, basil, black pepper, onion powder, olive oil, and Parmesan cheese, then mix well.

2. Add the shrimps and toss lightly until all the shrimps are evenly coated.

3. Preheat your air fryer at 350°F for about 3 minutes.

4. Place the coated shrimps in your air fryer's basket.

5. Cook the shrimps for about 8 to 10 minutes. Halfway through the cooking time, shake the basket to allow the shrimps to cook evenly.

6. Once cooked, transfer the shrimps to a serving bowl. Drizzle with half of the lemon and use the other half as garnish. Serve immediately.

Salmon with Dill Sauce

Yield: 4 servings

Ingredients:

For the Salmon:

- 2 salmon fillets
- 1 teaspoon olive oil
- Salt to taste

For the Dill Sauce:

- ½ cup plain Greek yogurt
- ¼ cup sour cream
- Salt to taste
- 1 tablespoon dill (finely chopped)

Directions:

1. Preheat your air fryer at 390°F for about 3 minutes.

2. Cut the salmon fillets into four portions. Pour a little olive oil onto each portion and sprinkle with salt.

3. Place the salmon fillets in your air fryer's basket and cook them for 7 to 8 minutes. Halfway through the cooking time, flip the salmon fillets to cook evenly.

4. While salmon is cooking, mix ingredients for dill sauce in a bowl.

5. When salmon is fully cooked, top salmon with sauce and serve warm.

Fried shrimp

Yield: 4 servings
Ingredients:

- 20 tiger shrimps
- ¼ teaspoon cayenne pepper
- ½ teaspoon old bay seasoning
- ¼ teaspoon smoked paprika
- Salt and pepper to taste
- 1 tablespoon olive oil

Directions:

1. Add shrimp, cayenne, seasoning, paprika, salt, and pepper to a bowl and mix until well combined.
2. Marinate in the fridge for 5 to 12 hours.
3. Preheat the air fryer to 390°F.
4. Add shrimp to the basket and fry for 10 to 15 minutes or until crispy.
5. Serve warm with a sauce of your choice.

Bacon Wrapped Shrimp

Yield: 5 servings

Ingredients:

- 10 pieces tiger shrimp (deveined)
- 10 slices bacon

Directions:

1. Wrap one slice of bacon around each shrimp, from the head of the shrimp to the tail.
2. Leave wrapped shrimp in the fridge for 30 minutes.
3. Preheat the air fryer to 390°F.
4. Add shrimp to the basket and cook for 10 minutes.
5. Drain shrimp of excess fat due to bacon.

CHAPTER EIGHT

Vegetables

When it comes to healthy living and balanced diets, vegetables are always an important element. Although starchy vegetables are avoided on keto, there is still a wide range of veggies you can add to your plate. Here are some tasty vegetable recipes to tickle your taste buds and fill your tummy.

Creamed Spinach

Yield: 2 servings

Ingredients:

- ½ teaspoon nutmeg (ground)
- 1 teaspoon black pepper
- 1 teaspoon salt
- 2 teaspoons garlic (minced)
- ¼ cup of Parmesan cheese (shredded)
- ½ cup of cream cheese (cubed)
- ½ cup of onions (chopped)
- 1¼ cup of spinach (washed, drained)
- Cooking spray

Directions:

1. Grease a heatproof pan that fits into your air fryer with cooking spray, then set aside.

2. In a bowl, combine all ingredients except the Parmesan cheese and mix well.

3. Pour the mixture onto the greased pan.

4. Preheat your air fryer at 350°F for about 3 minutes.

5. Place the pan into your air fryer and cook the creamed spinach for about 10 minutes.

6. After cooking, stir the mixture to blend all of the ingredients together.

7. Sprinkle with Parmesan cheese, then increase the heat to 400°F.

8. Continue cooking the creamed spinach for 5 more minutes until the cheese has melted.

9. Take the pan out of the air fryer and serve while hot.

Vegetarian Buffalo Wings

Yield: 4 servings

Ingredients:

- 2 tablespoons butter (melted)
- 2 tablespoons Frank's RedHot sauce
- 1 cauliflower head (cut into bite-sized pieces)
- Salt and pepper to taste
- Cooking spray

Directions:

1. In a bowl, combine the hot sauce, butter, salt, and pepper until well incorporated. Set aside.

2. Preheat your air fryer at 400°F for about 3 minutes.

3. Lightly grease the cauliflower pieces with cooking spray and place in your air fryer's basket.

4. Cook the cauliflower pieces for about 7 minutes. Halfway through the cooking time, shake the basket to cook evenly.

5. Transfer the cooked cauliflower pieces to the bowl with the sauce and toss to coat evenly.

6. Transfer the coated cauliflower pieces back into your air fryer's basket, then continue cooking for 7 to 8 more minutes until the cauliflower crisps up.

7. Once cooked, transfer the vegetarian buffalo wings to a plate and serve while hot. You can also serve this dish with a side of keto-friendly ranch dip.

Avocado Soup with Roasted Asparagus

Serving Size: 4 servings

Ingredients:

- 1 tablespoon garlic-infused olive oil
- 1 tablespoon ghee
- 1½ cups of asparagus
- 2 cups of vegetable stock
- ½ lemon (juiced)
- 1 medium-sized avocado (peeled, pitted, cubed)
- Salt and pepper to taste

Directions:

1. Preheat your air fryer at 390°F for about 3 minutes.

2. In a bowl, combine the asparagus, olive oil, salt, and pepper, then toss to coat evenly.

3. Place the asparagus in your air fryer's basket and roast for about 10 minutes. Halfway through the cooking time, shake the basket to cook evenly.

4. Transfer the roasted asparagus to a blender, along with the rest of the ingredients.

5. Blend until you get a smooth texture. Season with salt and pepper as needed.

6. Pour the soup into a sauce pot and warm over medium heat.

7. Serve immediately.

Asian-Style Roasted Broccoli

Yield: 4 servings

Ingredients:
- 1 teaspoon rice vinegar
- 2 teaspoons Sriracha sauce
- 1 tablespoon garlic (minced)
- 1½ tablespoons peanut oil
- 2 tablespoons soy sauce
- ⅓ cup peanuts (roasted, salted)
- 2 cups of broccoli (cut into florets)
- Salt to taste
- Fresh lime juice (optional)

Directions:

1. In a bowl, combine the broccoli, garlic, peanut oil, and salt, then toss until all the florets are evenly coated.

2. Preheat your air fryer at 400°F for about 3 minutes.

3. Place the coated broccoli florets into your air fryer's basket in a single layer, with some space in between. If needed, cook the florets in batches.

4. Cook the broccoli florets for about 15 to 20 minutes until crispy and golden brown. Halfway through the cooking time, shake the basket to cook evenly.

5. In a microwave-safe bowl, combine the rice vinegar, soy sauce, and Sriracha, then mix well.

6. Microwave the mixture for about 10 to 15 seconds until all ingredients are well-combined.

7. Once cooked, transfer the broccoli florets to a bowl. Drizzle with the sauce and toss to coat.

8. Add the peanuts and continue tossing until well combined. Drizzle with lime juice if desired and serve while hot.

Roasted Mushrooms

Yield: 4 servings

Ingredients:

- 1 pound mushrooms
- 2 tablespoons vegetable oil
- 1 teaspoon garlic (minced)
- 1 tablespoon mixed herbs
- Salt and pepper to taste

Directions:

1. Preheat your air fryer at 400°F for about 3 minutes.
2. Wash and cut mushrooms into halves.
3. Add to a bowl along with oil, garlic, herbs, salt, and pepper and mix until well combined.
4. Add to air fryer and roast for 10 minutes.
5. Serve hot, with a sauce of your choice.

Cheesy Asparagus

Yield: 4 servings

Ingredients:

- ½ cup grated parmesan cheese
- 2 tablespoons Italian seasoning
- ½ cup heavy cream
- 1 pound asparagus
- Salt and pepper to taste

Directions:

1. Preheat the air fryer to 400°F.
2. Remove the stems from the asparagus.
3. Whisk together the heavy cream, Italian seasoning, and parmesan cheese.
4. Place the asparagus in a dish. Cover with the cream mixture.
5. Place the dish in the air fryer and cook for 8 minutes.
6. Sprinkle the asparagus with salt and pepper before serving.

Cauliflower Fritters

Yield: 6 servings
Ingredients:

- 1 large cauliflower
- 1 tablespoon chili powder
- ½ teaspoon turmeric powder
- Salt to taste
- 2 tablespoons vegetable oil

Directions:

1. Boil the cauliflower and separate it into florets.
2. Add it to a bowl along with chili powder, turmeric, and salt, and mix until well combined. Allow it to stand for 1o minutes.
3. Preheat the air fryer to 390°F.
4. Brush oil over the cauliflower and add to the basket.
5. Fry for 10 to 15 minutes or until crispy.
6. Serve hot, with a sauce of your choice.

Roasted Parsnip, Celery, and Squash

Yield: 4 servings

Ingredients:

- 1 parsnip
- 3 stalks celery
- 2 small red onions
- 1 butternut squash
- ½ tablespoon fresh thyme
- 1 tablespoon olive oil
- Salt and pepper to taste

Directions:

1. Preheat the air fryer to 390°F.

2. Peel and cut onions into wedges. Peel the parsnip and cut it and celery stalks into cubes of 2 cm each.

3. De-seed butternut squash and cut into cubes.

4. Mix cut vegetables with olive oil and thyme and season.

5. Place seasoned vegetables in a basket and roast in the air fryer for 20 minutes. Mix vegetables once after 10 minutes.

6. When the timer goes off, check vegetables to see if they have turned brown.

7. Serve hot.

CHAPTER NINE

Dessert

There's nothing better than ending a delicious and satisfying meal with a sweet dessert. Yes, even while following the keto diet, you can enjoy dessert! In this last chapter, we will go through some mouthwatering desserts you can make right in your versatile kitchen appliance—the air fryer!

Chocolate Lava Cake

Yield: 1 serving

Ingredients:

- ⅛ teaspoon stevia
- ⅛ teaspoon vanilla extract
- ½ teaspoon baking powder
- 1 tablespoon butter (melted)
- 1 tablespoon golden flaxmeal
- 2 tablespoons cocoa powder
- 2 tablespoons water
- 1 egg
- Cooking spray

Directions:

1. In a bowl, combine all of the ingredients and mix well.

2. Pour the batter into a ramekin that you have greased lightly with cooking spray.

3. Preheat your air fryer at 350°F for about 1 minute.

4. Place the ramekin in your air fryer and bake for 8 to 9 minutes.

5. Once cooked, use tongs or oven mitts to take the ramekin out of your air fryer.

6. Allow to cool for a couple of minutes before serving.

Coconut Pie

Yield: 4 servings

Ingredients:

- 1½ teaspoons vanilla extract
- ¼ cup butter
- ½ cup coconut flour
- ½ cup powdered erythritol
- 1 cup of unsweetened coconut (shredded)
- 1½ cups of coconut milk
- 2 eggs
- Cooking spray

Directions:

1. In a bowl, combine all the ingredients, using a wooden spoon to mix everything together.

2. Grease a pie plate with cooking spray and pour the pie batter into it.

3. Preheat your air fryer at 350°F for about 3 minutes.

4. Place the pie plate into your air fryer and cook for about 10 to 12 minutes.

5. Halfway through the cooking time, check the pie to make sure it isn't burning. Use a toothpick to check for the pie's doneness and give the pie plate a turn to ensure it cooks evenly.

6. Once cooked, take the coconut pie out of the oven. Garnish with powdered sugar or shredded coconut and allow to cool before serving.

Fried Cheesecake Bites

Yield: 2 servings

Ingredients:
- ½ teaspoon vanilla extract
- 2 tablespoons powdered erythritol
- 4 tablespoons heavy cream (divided)
- ½ cup of almond flour
- ½ cup powdered erythritol
- 1 cup of cream cheese (softened)
- Cooking spray

Directions:

1. Line a baking sheet with parchment paper.

2. In the bowl of a stand mixer with a paddle attachment, combine the cream cheese, ½ cup of erythritol, 2 tablespoons of heavy cream, and vanilla extract, then blend until you get a smooth texture.

3. Scoop the cheesecake batter into the lined baking sheet.

4. Place the baking sheet into the refrigerator for about 30 minutes to firm up.

5. In a bowl, combine the almond flour with 2 tablespoons of erythritol. Set aside.

6. Take the baking sheet out of the refrigerator and cut the firm cheesecake batter into bite-sized pieces.

7. Dip each cheesecake bite in the remaining heavy cream, then roll them in the flour mixture.

8. Place the coated cheesecake bites on a plate, then grease lightly with cooking spray.

9. Preheat your air fryer at 300°F for about 1 minute.

10. Place the cheesecake bites in your air fryer's basket in a single layer. If needed, cook them in batches.

11. Cook the cheesecake bites for about 2 minutes. Halfway through the cooking time, shake the basket or flip the cheesecake bites over to cook evenly.

12.	Once cooked, transfer the cheesecake bites to a plate and serve.

Pumpkin Custard

Yield: 6 servings
Ingredients:
- 15 ounces pumpkin puree
- 4 eggs (beaten)
- ½ cup heavy cream
- 2 teaspoons pumpkin pie spice
- 2 teaspoons vanilla extract
- ½ teaspoon liquid stevia
- ½ teaspoon salt
- ⅓ cup whipped cream

Directions:
1. Preheat your air fryer to 325°F for about 3 minutes. Grease 6 ramekins.
2. In a large bowl, add all ingredients except whipped cream, and beat until smooth.
3. Divide the mixture evenly into prepared ramekins.
4. Place the ramekins in your air fryer and bake for about 30 minutes or until a toothpick inserted in the center comes out clean.
5. Remove the ramekins from the air fryer, and place on a wire rack to cool.
6. Serve warm or cold with a topping of whipped cream.

Blueberry Cobbler

Yield: 6 servings

Ingredients:

For Filling:

- 3 cups fresh blueberries
- ¼ teaspoon xanthan gum
- 1 teaspoon fresh lemon juice

For Topping:

- 2/3 cup almond flour
- 2 tablespoons butter, melted
- ½ teaspoon fresh lemon zest (grated finely)

Directions:

1. Preheat your air fryer to 350°F for about 3 minutes.
2. For filling, mix together all ingredients in a bowl.
3. Transfer the mixture evenly into a baking dish.
4. In another bowl, add all topping ingredients, and mix until a crumbly mixture forms.
5. Place topping mixture evenly over blueberry mixture.
6. Bake in the air fryer for about 18 minutes or until the top becomes golden brown.

Conclusion

The best way to follow the keto diet is to cook Ketogenic food at home. While there are now many keto-friendly food options in restaurants and shops, you can save a lot of money when preparing your own meals. Cooking at home ensures you only eat keto-friendly foods, allowing you to achieve ketosis and turn your body into a fat-burning machine.

Cooking on keto doesn't have to be challenging when you own an air fryer. With your air fryer, you can roast, grill, bake, and more. Creating tasty and healthy dishes is a breeze. With some practice, you can come up with more complex recipes to make your diet more interesting. Happy air frying!

Finally, I want to thank you for reading my book. If you enjoyed the book, please share your thoughts and post a review on the book retailer's website. It would be greatly appreciated!

Best wishes,

Melanie Bennet

* 9 7 9 8 2 0 1 1 3 8 4 2 4 *